Unravel

BY THE SAME AUTHOR

Bogman's Music (poetry)
Translations: Aistreann (novel)

Unravel

Tammy Armstrong

ANVIL PRESS | VANCOUVER

Printed and bound in Canada
Cover design: Rayola Graphic Design
Cover image: Clint Hutzulak

National Library of Canada Cataloguing in Publication
Armstrong, Tammy, 1974–
Unravel / Tammy Armstrong

Poems.
ISBN 1–895636–60–4

I. Title
PS8551.R7645U67 2004   C811'.6   C2003–907217–7

Represented in Canada by the Literary Press Group
Distributed by the University of Toronto Press

The publisher gratefully acknowledges the financial assistance of the B.C. Arts Council, the Canada Council for the Arts, and the Book Publishing Industry Development Program (BPIDP) for their support of our publishing program.

The Canada Council | Le Conseil des Arts
for the Arts | du Canada

BRITISH
COLUMBIA
ARTS COUNCIL
Supported by the Province of British Columbia

PUBLISHED BY
Anvil Press
P.O. Box 3008, Main Post Office
Vancouver, B.C. V6B 3X5   CANADA

This is for Joey

1. TRY NOT TO DISRUPT THIS DISTANCE

2. A COMMON VIOLET PRICKING THROUGH

WHEN THE WHITE NOISE DEAFENS

Earth will be warmer than we thought,
after all this circling.
—ANNE CARSON

1

TRY NOT TO DISRUPT
THIS DISTANCE

Accident Is a Language We Speak

You are an accident recurring
a misplaced suicide note
slipped by draft from the table
into cat's paw feckled air.

You are that last night inside the pub
swizzle stick drumming the table
buying rounds and rounds and rounds—
perpetually looping back:
the waitress and her tray
your thread-bare modesty.

Always balled
in one horse town boredom—
an inability to bruise egos, argue.

It goes no further
all my stories end with a denim jacket
an amble down my long drive
mongrel fingers trailing the hedges—
half-glance beneath finale skies.

I go no further.
These refusals have left me
disquieted
not attempting that spring morning funeral.
Please remember
we are all among the missing.

Moonies

In macraméed communities
Sun Myung Moon turned bungalow girls
into bacchanalian sister songs—
arsenals of commune off overgrown highways.

Not modest girls but lipsticked Lolitas
beveled from shopping malls
rural bus stops, docile
beneath the thumbs of accented Reverends.

There was evidence, my mother said:
school photos on shoddy mimeographs
staple gunned, jackknife pried
from power poles sentineled
among shade-dappled housing developments.

Too much suspicion: pamphlets, confessions
on the doormat, in the canned goods aisle–
Mother's hands soldered to cumbersome carts
our shape-shifting girl forms.

Cultists wanted the weak, the farmland misinformed:
in a haphazard Impala a butterscotch scented man
dragged a trunk of Britannicas
The world is so full, he said past the screen door
let me show you in these pages…

Parti Pris

Acquaintance of my sister's from Trois-Rivières
pulls swing–shifts at the donut shop
then manoeuvres her things out of my place
in Safeway boxes—ziggurats of second-hand.

Not yet noon, trunk hauled high
we suck down off sales
niggle small talk
out of weather forecasts, employment rates.

Him in the washroom, my sister says:
in 1977 his cousin was cheek down in a ditch of men
one didn't get away: crowbar, bare hands, boot stomped
8 mm paroxysm whirred through
a twenty-year incarceration.

Just out of Kingston
he dries his hands on my dish towel
tips the last of a lager into a glass
gives me space to lay down a verdict:

a clear bag of belongings, low-cinched belt
he hip-swaggered into 1997
cutting milk teeth on freedom
thread-ragged decades.

Premeditative, manslaughter, vigilante:
how dense is all that weight
the turnabouts in conversation
to satiate a monster deemed mild—
carbonated potential ripe in the sun.

Smoulder

Where did your grandfather think
he was going that night in the garage
hunched in the backseat nubuck of an Impala
horsepowered for broadsided nights
beyond crewel work corn fields.

And you, same age, decades later
atavistic in the cycle
with the white dog, White Album
cranked in your parents' garage—
bric-a-brac of years:
old bicycles, tool bench
musty skin of camp tents and tarps.

White dog didn't want to sleep
nosed your slackened bones like last call
dirty rag around your gin-frosted change.

If there is a next time
imagine us all as white dogs
nudging into gear shifts
into you, your grandfather
thirty-three years old—
rag doll pompadour of a world failed.

Try not to disrupt this distance
when you begin again
in a body too supple to be left
on planetary upholstery
barely worn through.

Widening Rifts

Community is a one armed man—
a ghost itch
where fingers once lifted Export A's
a Redbird match highlighted
hammer–chewed knuckles.

Tempered glass shattered
through thrush, culvert:
the stories fill in the blanks
the loss of young so and so
asleep at the wheel/drunk/stoned/pissed
they sat behind you in math class
poked dull leaded pencils into your spine
finally confessed a crush
a girl in another town.

Ghosts now
slipping through a windshield
bullet, iced lake
gone.

In this town the young don't survive.
The piper passes through often
takes them where coffee is fresh
where no one slips at the fish plant
almost seventeen
chewed slowly
mulled over.

Ignoring Newscast Exclusives

Step into the backyard
where the bulwark of collapsible chairs
remain as audience–empty seats
slung low to the undergrowth
where children are not bartered for
not 7–Eleven abducted
mothers do not slump over press conferences
begging drivers to return what's theirs—
no desiccated details of horror
what we're truly capable of.

De–construct:
down by the river, the provincial park coulée
with a salt bite of secluded hardpan—
only so much the heart–taut muscle can percolate.

Step into the backyard with circuitries
trowels, chew toys, roundhouses of storm—
the wind does unclench given time.
This premonition can clear the five–foot fence
ring an early morning door chime
wait for your fingers to pull back the curtains.

It owns time while loners are snatched
in torqued up muscle cars, luxury sedans
Playboy Bunny Econolines.
It's come to this: we disappear.

Step into the backyard because I fear your own finality
every bald–tired breakdown: a con artist in kid gloves.
I have fears of media scrimmages
blurred photos you wanted no part in
but I insisted for posterity: a greasy evidence.

I need your return
not a coffee mug left on the bookshelf
passport photos from a Thai visa
dog–earing your place in church sale paperbacks.
When you make the escape, smoke in well–lit atriums
leave the side door pubs early, stagger the line.

Drip Dry to Fredericton

Backpacks stocked
wool sweaters balled over high-tests
we hike out to the highway
thumbing Thursday afternoon
truckers on their way to the mill.

Some miles up the road
we take turns
thumbing, drinking in irrigation ditches—
smell of mulching leaves
dog shit spring surrounding.

Wrung from the saplings
always the sombre dirt paths
leading to places we've been raised to fear
where we call, *Can you see me now? Now?*
from behind tamaracks.

Crouching, pissing over boots
fighting through bramble
back to the Trans-Canada
diesel rumble of potential ride.

Mud scraped onto macadam
smiles, rearrangements of hair—
one hundred miles under a pullet angry sky
we race, a whim for freedom—
sixteen-year-olds, drip-drying our way to Fredericton.

Years After Charlotte Street

You come home to learn a language
internal
a frequency
because tradition is the aftermath
all the travel and photos mispronounced.

Remember when the door on Charlotte shifted
keeled stable
when the window hyper–extended
shattered one morning on the walk below:
in foreign spaces incidents replay
in a language
not dependent on poor construction
but the inevitable:
we leave because memory is short
and travel takes time
takes in our bodies:
separate countries
counter–clocking agendas
postcards that never match innuendos
the weather is fine, the food too spicy . . .

We are Northern shinbones
with migration in our blood
even after the passports are stamped heavy
and your phone rings and rings
when I forget where you've gone
how to convert currency into time.

Boston Bar New Year's

Another year tunneling
through a tail bone of ice
suspended off the Coquihalla:
elk crossings, cougar tramped paths
bonfire blisters mudding all that white.

This is where New Year's begins
where shadowed faces shimmy
caldera star diluvium
for a countdown, a disposition that says
tear here, begin again.

In a cabin the groundskeeper breathes rum
while lost dogs sleep
around his margin of bedding
pricking up for voices beyond the creek
cat spat of opened beers
ten, nine, eight . . .

Beyond the bark shorn sumacs:
no one to contend with
no one to peel back a sheer drape
to find the howler on their own front lawn
feet deep in a recycling crate
head thrown toward heaven
challenging the new year coming down
burning up before impact.

Grape Jelly

An entire Sunday
fingering grapes into torpid water—
jam making while her mother novice
jetted back to Oxford:
a nunnery, nest of prayer.

Concord raw
we stood two at the silver sink
separating pulp, eye–seed, skin
into bowls of recipe, procedure.

Relinquished now
her mother, unlinked
from little daughter
for rheumatic cottage pleasantries
tattered psalms.

To pray for a world . . .

My draft–lathed home barbs
her trail of smoke
while the night shaken out
like a weevil gnawed horse blanket
hesitates before the slow amble of descent.

Horse Girls

So you're a horse girl, he says,
smiles as though we are somehow afflicted
somehow convergent with dark rutted fantasy.

Yes, we are the ones who dream
in green and pale sparrow grass
who tick our tongues at the sunfisher
climb on, barely breathing
knowing fear could fill a field
snap a spine like tinder.

We ride bare–back
to watch the boys squirm
at the insistence in their minds:
we will always find something to hold on to.

Belly muscles quiver beneath our legs
while the struts of ribcage
large enough to envelope the sky–licked lake
carry us through backwater country
out to where we no longer hear the highway
no longer fear a moment with a gelding
a hatchback, car horn
something even the horse girls can't anticipate.

We know memory through tiger lily switchbacks
a tongue twist around a bit

a muzzle soft as deer moss, old denim
snuffling over a palm, searching
the horse girls who smell
of sunburn and barnyard dogs.

No longer half–women
we are extensions of broomtails
of Sable Island serenity
in love with no one
as we crawl easily over
urge the gate open with a tanned foot
gone while the light still holds above us.

Red Eye

You might have been home
watching PBS:
slow–drawl narration of carinal–spined Huskies
hauling sleds across the Arctic Circle—
the night a tuning fork hum
against frost–crusted windows.

Above power lines
I was in a Delphic belly
pulled across winter skies—
a child's toy
tethered to a thread–fine lace.

Suburbia swimming
we treaded the space above your neighbourhood:
avenues strung with light
bungalows—small eggs emitting reading lamp coronae.
Nosed toward the mountains
the engine moaned through my jaw bone:
theendtheendtheend.

Annulets over Hawthorne Street
the riveted dorsal fin
directed this soaring beluga toward star–beaded surface.
Thievishly, I searched through opal blush:
your television screen
the dogs running ice–mallet toed
forever toward pale glow
of an expected horizon.

Framing Up the Boathouse

Strakework as we see it
in the field off Jessy's Landing—
you and your father on the car hood
admiring the rib vault
of this skeletal blue whale
dry docked
rabbeted into placement

into cathedral solemnity:
a cast over the drive
sundials of shadow theatre
where time ambles
and we grow subtle.

Anchored to autumn's roofbeams
you, your father
speak in dusk lightened French
slipknotting the boathouse frame.

But outside the frame?
Do the geese continue cross bow migration
do the churned up fields continue to heal?
This slow capsized day
mattes with property stakes
a mulled Indian summer
and that cigarette passed
through shadow and light
from my fingers to yours.

2

A COMMON VIOLET PRICKING THROUGH

Furniture Crimes

I light a cigarette and adjust the window shade
there is a noise in the street growing fainter, fainter.
— RAYMOND CARVER

Ten years to the left
you scan my rooms for armoires, sofas, chesterfields:
words seeded into irreverence.
It wasn't deliberation, subscriptions to subtopia
it was a snowplow of progression
too many years without your shadow
over the double sinks
washing down the dregs of a cold coffee
tinkering with a back alley thought
beyond the Laundromat and Chinese grocery.
It was never a crave for manicured lawns
(I leave the forsythia petals where they fall
never rake the edges clean.)

In my dreams there is still room where we can smoke
a floor mattress, a crimp of sun
through bed sheet curtains.
The neighbours wake slow there
no one drags out
mohawk lawn sprinklers from sheds
to spit minutes off the day.
We burrow into dewy air

thankful someone has forgotten
how to pay mortgages
that we are still astral shots
beneath renovated roofs
a slow descent of language
into Saturday morning nothing.

City of Dogs

Here is a situation rehearsed:
an afternoon shower
a face in a band of spray
the survival kit beneath the work bench
sealed in tupperware among puddling water mains
hung high from the rafters—
this house sleeps above a city of liquid soil
uprooted, stewed
splintering appendages, trees like jackstraw girders
each a cursory symbol of this green green city
all of its accordion creases.

Near Chinatown, a woolpack of spice
bottle rockets, chest–heaves
ribbons of sound into the dust–hewn sky
aftershocks, aftermath.

San Andreas: a camphor sting of paranoia
a good bottle of Havana Club, an e–mail letter
love, long distance
from the fault line
the parade moves on
an anthem of dogs runs down.

Bugbears—When the Drum Tilted

I.
Something to be said about basements
a misconstrued ambivalence—
neglected parental birthdays
that leavened silence
during pre-holiday phone calls.

It's the must of dove-tailed paperbacks
sour grass rot of mower blades
the suspended angst: this clutter breathes.

My hands wing walls
for misplaced light switches
spider shadows that pull familial away.

Outside this door:
children with double dutch songs
the thwack of measuring tapes
as handymen rebuild a porch.

But the basement is an egg-eating snake
a silent devourer.
Spin the dial. Make it stop.

II.
Make it stop. In the backyard
where neighbours question my ability
to burn the wasp nest clean
compost the piñata of mud and paper
give up this hymn of bees
their flights through the basement door.

Knackered bodies—mandorla smooth
beat uselessly against garden level windows
crawl over the tool bench
something sweet on the tin of turpentine
on the last ache of western light
severing an amber beer bottle
a tonguing of pale ale warmed
inside its base
inside all this dank exhale.

Antiques Road Show

How many knick-knacks have they assessed:
chipped figurines smuggled sock-balled
in post war duffels
all this bric-a-brac moved
through generations into a gamut
white noised programming.

Neoclassics from fire sales, estate auctions
mantelpieces ticking a notice
span of pendulum
a history among erudite knowledge
two hundred years of heirloom knock-offs.

Can the shelves fill
leaving no space for soft-spoken hosts to hold?
These trinkets have lasted generations of children
marital arguments that clamoured for breakage
the cool abjection palm cupped
the resonance of good china, willow print
triangulated on the linoleum floors.

In my home: low-key drama epoxyed pieces
fine cracked gifts from dollar stores
Chinatown wicker emporiums
a cheated heritage, a moot collection.

The Uselessness of Stolen

A clarinet version of *Rhinestone Cowboy* trickled
like gutter rain through speakers as the aisle search began.

We came to Newberrry's for objects never needed—
a stick of mood lip balm
a hair band, translucent, blue gem in a sunbeam.
Our nails painted in last week's gloss
pecked over Chinese pencils
the wood too soft to hold grey leads for long—
all slipped into windbreakers
pockets filled softly.

Newberry's Department was throw rugs, knitting yarn
and a seven-stool diner beside the hair products
the pensioners smoking over coffees
over the din of the dish machine
the shank of Muzak.

Afterwards
sprinting through the automatic doors
past the quarter-fed carousel horse
beaming a fibreglass grin
we thumped through to the outside
our whirligig bodies, uneven with booty, high on crime.

We were ten, maybe twelve
with fingers objects stuck to:
the uselessness of stolen.

A trove to pull out, examine on a Sunday afternoon
like the plastic tiara you wore for the mirror
asking, *When do you think they'll forget?*

Unclaimed Ten Million Dollar Lottery Ticket

Somewhere in the Kootenays
there's a ticket, quartered
in a spend–thrift's smooth leather wallet
mushing amidst fabric softener wash—
fish–eyed porthole at the coin laundry
everyone oblivious to the succession of numbers
sequestered from anniversary and birth dates
locker combinations from grade nine gym.

Somewhere a man leans over
the hull of a four–cylinder
spark plugs, oil pan
calculating when a trade–in is too late.

There's romance in the carpal tunnel cashier
wrists corseted in support
wondering how anyone spends fifty bucks on snacks:
cakes and fruit leather, incandescent gel bowls.

Let it not be
someone with a multi–car garage
a gardener and working knowledge of bull markets.

Let it be a dollar store Polaroid
cheque number mug shot
chain–hearted grin
hands still blackened with axle grease—
the unfettered smugness of the underdog done well.

Why I Don't Own Garden Gnomes

In between bearded pots of moss
cedar planters dragged from the sunken fence
to fill space, hide neglected dead heading
there is no gnome sentinel.

No concrete beard, slouched knickerbockers
that make me think we've encountered this before:
the man pushing a cart down Hastings Street
the Santa fear so many children share.

Inconspicuous smile beneath the barren pear
while the dog kowtows to taproots.
In my garden there are no overseers of beddings
fire sale perennials, burgeoning weeds.

In my garden it's difficult to tell what's beyond
the rhubarb fronds: soothsayer house cats
padding foreign territory
slim infants tucked into cracker barrels.

Kansas State Trailer Park

Victims in Bermuda shorts, shower thongs
roll with the punches,
stagger hyperboles where a scrawl of tornado
unspooled leavings of timber and insulation.

Why haul another trailer through Mid-East velum
or crouch another year below the dinette
while winds scour low-rent housing
in the uvula of corn fields?

Not pandemonium but acceptance:
mother nature spring cleans
god doesn't like mobility.

The representatives are gone
the co-operative search called off
for wedding photos, child's shoes.
Now dogs roam dark grins
haul batting from toys
lick the broken eggs dry.

All of it picked clean, weltered
until the next mis-keyed prediction:
sloe-eyed twisters demanding
engagement rings, tupperware
the burl of resurrection.

Earmark

On the derelict side of the lake
tree town, bone town, engines up on front yard blocks
a buzz needles slick captions from laminated binders.

The tattooist
arms havocked by Looney Toons, scripture:
a stint up in Renous
maximum security raw
is all business, Polysporin
pausing only to swab with gauze
admire ink bands ridging a vein.

Macaws penned from ankle to thigh
the wife trounces through smoked-out rooms
inhabiting a sanctuary of jungle:
an exodus of ocelots, tapirs
along her boomerang shoulder blades.

At the kitchen table
booze-shot teens like random strains of music video
soon humble beneath the needle—
inked out wells waiting for the hurt to sink down.

Baby

My mother says:
you're not maternal
too set in your ways.
Lover of solitude,
emptied into spit shined freedom.
No small voiced questions, responsibility
to teach walking, alphabets.

So I spend my money on books, instant noodles.
I change topics because you have not written
do not know my nuances
my Rikki–Tikki–Tavi love
for animals
for anything stray.

Waiting for the Punch-line

My father, drunk in the Adirondack
blurs Navy stories:
Baltic leagues, deep sea fishermen
the dolphins that torpedoed crests
chaperoned carriers through winter squalls.

And finally the blue fish
snared in brine-shot skein
perched on the deck like a bowling trophy
a headlight bobbing between its eyes—
ambassador to fault line canyons.

Primordial in its reminder:
outside shore leave, the women
the eventualities
men return to small towns
minds rowdy—
empties clashing around the gas pedal
the delinquent shenanigans
composted astride boyhood
but the blue fish becomes parable

becomes bow-legged time
standing on the front lawn as we do
calling fathers with fathers home to supper
Saturday afternoons
drunk in a suburban stain
while the ocean still creates

a new species every ten days
embryonal in black strap depths—
something welcoming
the pure nocturne of repetition.

Unkempt Days of the Roofer and His Children

In the muffler shot wagon
aluminum ladder strapped to the roof
they come before eight o'clock:
the wife, the husband, the boy
on the lawn
spinning a shadow while they unload.

Maybe he should visit the grocer
whose children play, popsicle-stained
behind the counter, the lottery kiosk
a barrier for suction cup gun brigades.

But inside this bare-armed morning
the roofer's son carries the light end of ladders
with his mother: loose breasted, beautifully run-down.

A nowhere summer vacation:
a back seat piled high with tool belts, tin clippers
strangers in stranger's yards
shielding his eyes, watching his father climb
the long bones of childhood
succumbing to a lace-work of scaffolding.

The view his father explains at dinner:
this city of green and blue
a parabola of ocean to make the mind spin
perk balance up into a body trussed

each moment synchronized with each bend
of fractured light on the tailspin of gulls.

❧

Father, roofer
stilted tan mellowed by September
rebuilds the chimney
scrapes mortar over jet–streaked afternoons.
There are mantras of disposition to fall through, he says
my brother slipped from a height
of enviable boredom, routine.

Not spiders but men who forget they're scaling
rooftops, the hot copper bite of steeple
those shingled pages in a roofers' bible:
never be too confident
always one step away
from stratospheric blue . . .

For a Prowler

Come around the side where the winds hit hardest
southerlies have cracked that glass-smattered stucco
beneath the grapevine
shot thick with morning glory.

Watch the pergola's cedar shims
ankled with creeping charlie, variegated and low
in the yard the hydrangea waits—
hall monitor with its thoughts elsewhere.

On the porch, mind the moss slicking the steps
there's nothing arbitrary
about slim carpetings
holding in what's left of the rains.

Finally, adjust to the dimness:
a woman inside
this soap opera cluttered afternoon
waiting for your footsteps to climb then stop.

Prince Albert Street

There's a rat problem—
fat rumped creatures pattering
the clothes lines, telephone wires
thick with the leavings
from the Korean restaurant dumpster.

The shut-in over the back fence
collects strays, one-eyed Toms:
rats and cats traipsing territory.

Where to go when the young couple fights
with the windows open
late night arpeggio
finger-pointing
shadows overhead, leaping into trees.

Houses Down

2003

Not the malleable skeletons of children but jersey cows
the neighbour, plied with whisky, says
beneath the broken ceramic, stubby beer bottles
cows are buried.

In my backyard . . .

a geological cut away
deep enough
for fits of sod and soil
a tangling of earthworms . . .

In ancient African villages bodies are found
spooned, nautilus in each others' bones
cross-hatched above the hardpan.

Here above the placement
layers of baritone
as my nephew chases the dog
as I carry magnolia transplants

into the seam of light
at the edge of the house.

What else sleeps below our feet?
If we spade cleanly through
to severed tap roots
sprouts that crown the ether dry
the cattle bones' butchered scrawl:
block lettered, open vowel, syllabic
beneath late–night bonfires
where we burned the old fence down.

Messages we're missing
intaglio we're still too self–absorbed to decipher.

1942

Not seraglios, opium dens
but Mission–style, Arts and Crafts homes
with lantern jaw porches—
encumberments of history
infantry men turning deadbolts
to gopher Norman soils.

When they closed the eyelet curtains
they shut out the light

Japanese fishermen craved:
past interned fence lines
fingers twined a netting of air
prepared an exodus
through jagged northern canines—
the anthropology of residence.

These were the widow walks
the xenophobic
corduroy streets perambulating
strains of accent
across a dairy land
cow town, fish town
while the men networked warrens.

Manure on the upwind
women cupped udders
thought of foxhole boys
who missed the edge of milk trains moving east.

These women hovered hands over the bath mirror
gauging transformations:
dairy women
with ammonia stung musculature
couldn't force
a knitting of irregular purls
talc the babies—
thunderheads of fatherless children
chamois a hinge of land.

1940

In a Leningrad bathhouse
he contracted polio—
one leg refusing
twisted into water-logged teak.

Friends supine in iron lungs
listened to mothers read war efforts
Trotsky's dry-throated assassination
the spellers with proletarian illustrations
apple cheeked children
dogs that obeyed.

An immigration song:
years later with children and wife
the Russian in a wheelchair
tinkered over tool tables
smuggled husbands through the root cellar
for Siberian vodka
cigarettes sent out for.

Accent like a burl of tundra
a rigging of ice floe
before a mainland collision
demanded knockings of drink
Black Nun tobacco swaggered
from a tightened fist.

This is fifty years inside the house:
a relic of a church key
snapped at the head
a peephole onto the street
where the drug cartels marketed
the muscle cars sashayed.

Salk couldn't predict
post–vaccinal compromises:
polio creeping up the spine
a half–century later
a hoar–frost paralysis
pride punched confession:
the wheelchair an extension
an awkwardness of dance
with two feet strapped in.

He again became
the fear of summer–tempered children
the suspicion of soured milk
manoeuvrability of oxygen—
unsustainable quarantine.

Loose–jowled short falls:
a squeak of wheel
soft scrape of a child–sized foot
edging a chair to the window.

1982

Women fawn–limbed pace the street—
thin bones balanced
above stiletto predilection
jack–rabbit men
who demand with Fisher–Price car seats
department store portraits windowed in a wallet.

They are the late nights of Prince Albert Street:
refugees who thought
Vancouver asylum
not a skeletal system of compromise.

But neighbours fill soup cans
with grapeshot and stones
blackball tinted windows
follow the women
cause sores to fester a craving
slick down a throat
numb the marrow that keeps them returning.

In a neighbourhood of poppy gardens
yellow booted children stomp the puddles clear
calling, *is that car number five for you today?*

The girls teeter, think shelters
hot chocolate the mission vans offer
if only they'd stand still long enough

for a white sheeted sermon
a sandwich bitter with mustard, proposition.

2003

Not *boat people* but merchants
who speak broken English
finger calculator adjustments
wink as they return change.

In one shop I look for pasta
What do Canadians like? she asks
hands me an egg
deep, fossilized—
an embryo tight
in fermented calabash.

Cold in my palm
the weight of hibernation:
to bite through small bones
peel apart flightless wings . . .

Outside her children sing
oxymoron, oxymoron, you're an oxymoron.

After closing
when the flats of bananas, jackfruit are stored
do they dream
a South China Sea palate

the hurl and pitch of a wooden boat
knocking the vertebrae of waves
serrated like pirates
who sent daughters and sisters
to brothels along the coast.

Do they hear the chafe of ribbing
the boat ready to capsize
thunderheads of fatherless children
against a dark hinge of rain.

What do Canadians like?

❦

All the dreams come back to this:
stepping to the floor each morning
waiting for the swells to subside
surprise in how agile the children move
through the galley kitchen
the floor merely a floor.

Their English broadsides
iconographic as a mother tongue now.

But this soil will not heave
their bones will not be pye–dog snapped
there is room to stretch
stretch out their arms
recite a history.

Ice Storm

Cuffed in hail the silver birches knuckle
until hollow tibias shatter marrow-rotten sap
a tire swing sustainability
a bile-struck sparrow's nest beneath fingerlings of twig.

❧

Not canals within the Beaufort Sea but backyards
salad gardens draped in post-wedding contortions
patio furniture leaned into indecipherable letterings.

❧

This is a heaven
ravaged with thrush
moving as nomadic stations
along the hills:
dew claws at windows
cracking shin bones
the trees amputate.
The ice storm expands.

❧

Ravens are finally appreciated—
apostrophes hung low in the east
blackness to keep the white piked down

augured deliverance, interpretation
thermal scalded flight feathers
of shadow hawks who eye snowshoe hares
the rest and fall of prints along the berm
the sun's reluctance to thaw the sky.

❧

There will be colour again
a common violet pricking through
another season—
a passing, collective overture.

Ice

Solid enough on the lake
to walk across that November
school cancelled morning
your boots have new treads to pull
you across to the centre
always the centre with you—
to half–dead trees—
hub of landscape holding steady.

Stretch out your tongue
taste the damp birch moments
reminding you:
be part of it all
never far from a slow beat
of frozen surface
the cataract that blinds nothing
as you, lone figure
skate circles of your own.

Coyote

Territorial further than the cool pitch
of Queen Elizabeth Park
or coifed lawns of the North Shore:
coyotes hold a nimbus of street light
wade the row house hosta borders.

In the tamed city—
parboiled chicanery
tongue–scalded yips
as they trowel backyards
sap below softwood pickets
with the fortitude of burglars, home wreckers.

They are wall–eyed castrati mewls
calla lily eared:
this city spoons in, runs out
hedge–ways through property lines
the hackles of street work pylons.

Look beyond the front steps:
a shadow
late sun matted
piebald and hungry.

Trespasser at the empty milk bottles
the neglected paper boy circulars
twined up with slim elastic
before the wind catches and spreads.

In the morning against the fence
an evidence:
strew of compost
recycling tins tongued off patios.

Canis latrans, coyotl
Aztec trickster four–pawed
leaves consonantal etchings—
house cats draped unceremoniously
in a city suspected of sleep
where bath–robed owners bend
to smooth damp fur
glimpse down cul–de–sacs
for their own limbless gin–trapped trust.

3

WHEN THE WHITE
NOISE DEAFENS

For the Sake of All Insomniacs

Houses, you know, grow stubborn
easily when you strip them bare.
—George Seferis

Where the rest of the world is cast off
just past the 3 a.m. bonfire
slug ravished spinach plot
we've been given time to forget.

Time for all those we love who have parents
on morphine drips in dark rooms
off the kitchen, *sotto voce* of 80–proof tragedy
we're still awake, fingers blackened.

For the sake of all insomniacs down the block
who watch infomercials with the sound low
who call lonely operators only too happy
to sell microwave bacon crispers
rhinestone C&W.

We come through phone lines, open windows
with songs remembered from grade school
with howls to move the damn dog
from the belly of the fire—
spine shimmying recoil.

We are here, lawn chairs drawn tight
snapping piles of burning fence
celebrating those who ran out
out of time, things to say
their own pickets years too soon.

Ba-lu and the Beaver

Laurentian winter and Ba-lu jackknifing through.

To want something that badly . . .

They watched him from the window
through the ice:
a footing and that beaver whip-tailing.

To stay out there all day says something.

The dog was frayed by sundown
exhausted
hypothermic salation
still refusing
        a stalemate, white flagged surrender.

Call it stupidity, obsessiveness

but rugged determination
is cottage country
all the regulars at the tavern
standing hands in pockets
a rommelpot bellow

        *come in from the cold
                from the god damn cold.*

Only so much blood
so much fish–tailed time
and the ice holds only one promise
for a near–dead dog
piss and lake sodden
welts raised into fierce Braille.

Somnambulistic, Ba–lu
limb–twitches closer:
the dam with its alcoves and catacombs
romance in the surviving
a language we were all born to read.

Barcelona Boys

The neighbours in new soccer shoes
poke cut mango through the tines of the cage
teach their parrot Spanish
vivimos en la ciudad
but the bird merely squawks
a migraine of polysyllabic babble
thick–accented.

He will not cooperate
will not peck the fruit from Safeway
breathe this moss–tinged air
but dreams a wingspan
a hemispheric envelopment:
not *ciudad* but jungle
where pin feathers scatter dust paths
after flight cradles instinct
not around the world
with compartmental ownership
but merely to the spires
to overlook
what has always been above, around
just waiting to be rediscovered:
fruit familiar on the rind.

African Grey

Eight years after
his sister–in–law smuggled
a clutch of chicks from Mexico

the bird became a divorce settlement
caged on top of the refrigerator
until one evening

home from the pub
it made its escape.
Greetings Comrade

the only words learnt: clubfooted mimicry
of telephone lines, fingerprinted laughter
the slam of the cupboard door.

Walking home from the cove
how to explain . . . three years
burdock of autumn chill

and out of this came
Greetings Comrade
from a stranger's window.

How that woman mistrusted
his midnight excitement
his persuasion of property.

He and the conversationalist
long after the wife went mainland
evenings were fine
pecking at the cage, saying nothing new.

Jellyfish at the Peruvian–Chinese Wedding

Simple as when we test for wind direction
the taste of coast line—
these wet-finger, slickened Ming bowls
staked like beach fodder
trailing red tide toxins
for now have ended on the buffet.

We do not eat jellyfish, I say
meaning the east coast, myself in plural;
still guests ladle the iridescent ribbons
spin lazy susans for left-overs—
sun-bleached jade sauce
as though the bride's bracelets softened.

Two hundred guests, four translators
tongue a glistening of salt and marinara—
the rock-stranded, barnacle-maimed:
a flesh that exposes storm clouds
spooled over capstans.

Fifteen courses poached red and gold:
high above Chinatown, the darkened market streets
we applaud uncles
who lead out dance floor flower girls
sheeny palms and cheeks
wiped like sailors' over crinolines.

Contortionist

We should all be born with the ability to fold inward
paper cranes, cicadas smooth creased
a sea urchin of origami suffering—
slight touch pin curled
to our bodies, our vulnerable flexion
because neighbours are diagnosed too young
with exponential metastasis
and mothers seethe singular mid–life crises
over dating service perambulations.

❧

But spindle–shanked,
the contortionist bends still.
She is Plato's intact flatfish:
placing ankle over wrist
while we envy alone
scar tissued, solitary, maimed
punished for misappropriating body language
the way we weave our arms over our chests

when lovers go
knotted, disfigured
focus on the walk–away
damning these bodies
for not collapsing soft corners
folding into something
less resembling a mis–matched half
sturdy but reckless.

While You Were in Mongolia

I took to the track—
the all thumbs fumble
horses, urgency slick
tantivy with escape.

Beer held tight
we manoeuvred
announcers' squawks:
Hastings Park
scarved in hand–rolled smoke

Those cinder–blocked afternoons
kept the mind monosyllabic—
a single vowel of horse track:
u, u
u, u . . .

I think I'll buy you socks
with my winnings—
this handful of change
counted near the concessions
the cankerous din
of slow motion replay.

Stakes: history of the underdog
in the field where we all reeled
stoned inside this circulet mountain range
my small change:
damp tokens to kill
time, those moments between
when the white noise deafens.

Iona Beach

Cedar chipped alleys
between Richmond's airport and sewage plant
where it's *perfectly safe*, they say
but the machinery, mountains of damp bark . . .

The only word I think, *termite*
all of this moving just beyond
where the dog licks shoreline swellings
no one crouches as the planes come in

nor shields their eyes, creates visors
from steepled fingers:
let the planes land smoothly
not tailspin in sputtering protest—
wooded impact, minor casualties.

Signs say bird sanctuary, beware of camouflage
but aren't we always moving this way
a possibility the Retriever
driftwood trapped in its jaws
might pick up the scent of my cigarette downwind
the fruit of my shampoo and turn.

Where do we go then? Which way to run:
sink deep in low tide carpets of muck and mussel
or toward the tarnished platter of water.

Like my dog who paddles foam and debris
turning, waiting
this is the only way out.

Hagiography

S gives me a book of saints:
paragraphs of suffering
pyres, dismemberment
the willingness to do it all again.

But this house demands
attention like a distempered child
and we frequently unravel
rarely meet saints anymore.

Payments are high
wallets get lost
inside seams
bar booths while we hide
around an amber pitcher
planning that final trip out
in the inherited Impala
the mammoth ferry lowing in the cove.

But the dog needs shots
I have a dental appointment on Friday
the kind you can't ignore
the kind that abscesses
until you sign for the extraction
and still masked, the dentist allows you to palm
the small white tooth

harmless now with its rivulets of blood
still solid
not bending when pressed
between the pages of a book of saints
not even under that kind of pressure.

There are Thousands of Ways to Find Attention:

The neighbour has tendencies—
pulped heart whimpering
from a small corner of chest cavity
fire trucks outside, impatient.

Drawn and quartered, sun still down
cherry lights serrate
another ice–plaqued morning
a bubble spin of spent time.

I'm afraid of him as reminder—
age, stairs, the indecency of canes,
hop o my thumb
tormented gait
toward the bus stop
the tick of immigrant Fraser Street.

The procession is slow
reflective vests, overwrought chest X's
blurb of vindictive siren—
parenthesis to the old blue house
where his lover is careful
to turn out the porch light
before warming the car
tailgating ambulances.

The Hill Where It Sits

Candied air glosses the town
spins sugar over the closed–down shops
the trucks rolling toward the scales
for one last load of wood chips.

For years, the chocolate dippers
have worked here—
hands running faucets of sucrose
over maraschino nibs
bricks of nougat.

These women, oblivious now
to the jelly bean rattle of a hopper
squirrel sticks of cinnamon in their pockets
lemon drops down cotton sleeves.

These hunched women are responsible
for the children
BMXing through gold plated afternoons
small town gulches
an empty Lofood parking lot.

All waiting
for the factory on the hill to release
the hair netted figures
a scented twelve-hour shift assembly line
moving down into the town—
street lights just beginning
to acknowledge the day's end.

After Snake River Canyon Jump

Was there a time mid–air to recollect
the years, the women, incorrigible flight
over burnt out trucks, radial tires?

It was never the idea of launching but landing
the ability to strike a pose, let the rhinestones
glitter to envy flashbulb spray.
Ovations in your name
at the lips of every kid with a BMX, oil barrel.

Now talk–show mornings, kitchen clock hum
accentuate the state of your liver
rivered with infection
the cheapening of Wild Turkey
sump oil apothecary.

This stilted charade, old man
arc welded between the bourbon and a nap—
nostalgia close–captioned
red, white and blue.

The rest clings
carefully chosen vistas
out of retirement complexes
a bathroom mirror moment:
feet slipped from kick pegs
but a hell grip on the handlebars.

Kick Peg

Tepid when I mention
that morning on the bike
cutting lane after lane
until seared from a careless right turn
my knee contacted
a back fender bent into silver right angles.

You reached
         reflex, instinct
ensure it's one piece
where would we be if I'd lost it?

A tap–hop into the bedroom each night
our ability to curl close into new space
keep all that other cauterized.

Would you buy me skirts
to keep my wardrobe equilateral
natural as I stork balance
unfastening
clips and zippers.

Then.
Slow crawl across the bedding
back to where we might dream
the motorbike, the steamy morning
we ran away.

Pretend our heads are connected by a string.
My chest to your spine
in tandem
the city miniaturized in rearview mirrors
your hand reaching still
over calf and knee
this skeletal Braille:
a reassurance, collateral.

Shelter

There were at least thirty
and her in Wellingtons through the muck
disassembling the scrum—
muzzles punctured
half–healed pelts—
stiff with clay and shit.

The dog lady took on marauders
the street smart, abandoned
jinxed child companions.

Through a knot hole I watched her
step over the pariahs
scrape mud back in search
for my description:
consistent, consistent.

Deep in the woods
her halfway house neighbour
took air rifle pot shots.
Pressed to the chicken wire
this hell–bent motley
of valley–roamers, poultry killers
harboured no escape.

Man's best friend:
left on the side of highways
knocked around with a length of chain
that one has clear eyes, she said.
Take that one.
He pads gently still
easily repaired.

Reducing Speed

Half–glance from the highway into villages
broad–chested haze of a television
the idea of children
bellied down on a carpet . . .

Knock on a door
insist on a cup of tea in an oversized mug
in a kitchen still lemon heavy
with washed dishes, floor cleaner.

Backpack at your feet
faint hiss of plastic in your boots.
Sit and listen to weather knuckling windows
solipsistic drive-by–weary rain on high beams.

Would you tell them about misguided exits
the men on ATV's who yelled
Where you from, cowboy?
There is property, territorial heritage
an opus of Legion Hall travel guides.

On the shoulder, a three–legged spaniel named Tripod
escorts you through red–eye warning
while a squad car sidles up fifty dollar fines
for your thumb extended through cataract blizzards.

Walk or drive there's no middling here—
the houses set too far back to see
all that impassioned illumination:
age and age well. The world may run you down.

ACKNOWLEDGMENTS

Many thanks to all those who kicked platitudes out
the door and listened to my rants after an earlier
version of this collection was stolen in Halifax.
Michelle Doherty, Johannn Tienhaara, Christine
Davidson, Shawn Reynar, Rob Bennett, Naheed Khan,
Sara McNeice, Erin Kastner, Joey Babineau and my
mother, Carol for so much love and phone calls.

Some of these poems have appeared in: *Pedestal
Magazine, Nth Position, Forget Magazine, The Fiddlehead*
and *Coastlines: The Poetry of Atlantic Canada*.

Thanks to Brian Kaufman and everyone at Anvil
who encouraged with their honesty and bawdy
humour.

"Grape Jelly" is for Erin. "For the Sake of All
Insomniacs" is for Naheed and Rob. "Ice" is for Cid.

Tammy Armstrong's debut collection of poetry, *Bogman's Music* was shortlisted for a Governor General's literary award. She currently lives in Halifax where she is an ESL teacher.